CINCINNATI TODAY

CINCINNATI TODAY
A Portrait in Color

Photographed by J. Miles Wolf

Cincinnati's new performing arts center, the Aronoff Center for the Arts.

FOREWORD

For those of us lucky enough to be living here in Cincinnati, we see the forms and shapes and colors of our town every day, but I'm not really sure we ever look at them.

The same buildings and bridges and parks and streets...they wear many faces, evoke many moods...all dependent on how the sun shines or how the shadows fall. Is there a mist or a torrential downpour? Perhaps a night's light casts a reflection that you could swear "was never there before!"

It's a beautiful city, and once you think you've seen it all, along comes Miles Wolf, his God-given eye giving his camera almost a vision of its own...and we see Cincinnati as we've never seen it before...and it's a joy, which is what you'll feel when you peruse these pages of the wonderful and talented mind's eye of Miles Wolf. Enjoy it. It's our town.

—Jerry Springer

First Edition, 1991.
Second Edition, 1993.
Third Edition, 1995.
Fourth Edition, 1996.
Fifth Edition, 1998.

ISBN 0 9647433-0-2

Captions by Professor Daniel Ransohoff

Wolf Publishing Company
708 Walnut Street
Cincinnati, OH 45202
(513) 381-3222

1-800-492-5105
Printed in China through Palace Press

Delta Queen homecoming.

Right, Riverboats line the bank of the Ohio River during Tall Stacks.

Union Terminal interior mosaic murals depicting the development of the region. The murals were designed by Winold Reiss.

Right, Union Terminal, the former train station now houses the Cincinnati Natural History Museum and the Cincinnati Historical Society. The building is one of the finest examples of art deco architecture in the country.

Following pages, the Cincinnati Bengals.

Mt. Adams shrouded in morning fog.

Left, Lytle Park, Taft Museum, and Mt. Adams.

Saturday afternoon, around the Tyler Davidson Memorial Fountain.

Left, "The Genius of Water", Tyler Davidson Memorial Fountain.

Xavier University.

Left, the University of Cincinnati, "the bridge" and McMicken Hall.

Mirror Lake and Krohn Conservatory, Eden Park.

Riverbend Music Center, home to the Cincinnati Pops Orchestra also hosts the top acts in Rock, Country and Jazz.

The world-renowned Cincinnati Symphony Orchestra, seen here at Music Hall, celebrated its Centennial with a major European tour in 1995.

Jungle Trails, Cincinnati Zoo and Botanical Gardens.

The Cincinnati Zoo is world renowned for the breeding of white tigers.

Following pages, Festival of Lights, elephant house, Cincinnati Zoo.

Ohio River and Mt. Adams on a golden Fall day.

The Boathouse at Sawyer Point Park houses a world-class rowing training center and the Montgomery Inn Restaurant.

Following pages, "Light Up Cincinnati" from the Daniel Carter Beard Bridge.

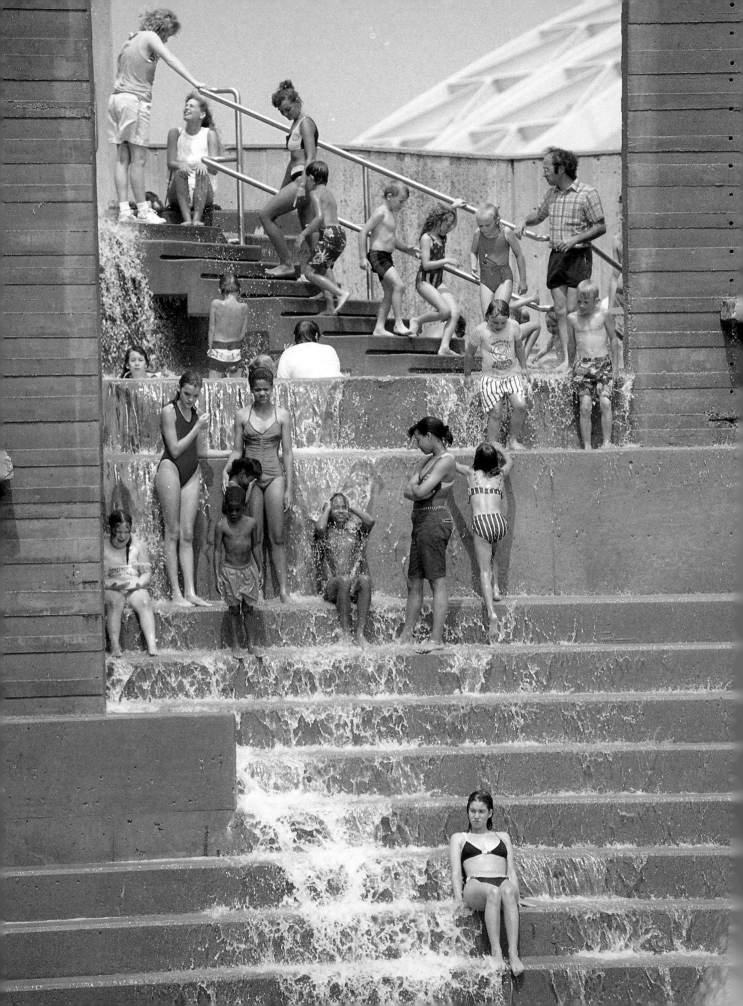

Sawyer Point Park and the Procter and Gamble Pavilion, site of the Black Family Reunion Festival.

Left, Water fountain, Yeatman's Cove.

Following pages, Riverfest fireworks.

A sold-out crowd, 1988 All-Star Game, Riverfront Stadium.

National League Championship Series.

Below, the 1990 Reds celebrate a World Series victory.

Serpentine Wall, sunrise.

Serpentine Wall with the Ohio River at flood stage.

Following pages, St. Paul, Old St. Mary's, Music Hall, Union Terminal.

Over-the-Rhine.

Left, Music Hall, designed by Samuel Hannaford, built in 1878, is home to Cincinnati's symphony, opera, ballet, and May Festival.

Following pages, Ohio River overlook, Eden Park.

Ault Park Pavilion.

Mt. Storm gazebo, "Temple of Love".

Right, Gazebo in Eden Park.

Captain George Stone House, 1880, High Victorian style, Hyde Park.

Plum Street Temple, built in 1866, was completely restored in 1995.

Hamilton County Court House, built in 1919.

Cincinnati City Hall (right), designed by Samuel Hannaford, completed in 1893.

The new Bradford Eastman Phillips Hall at the Cincinnati Art Museum, Eden Park.

Right, Cincinnati Art Academy.

Covington, Kentucky, is one of the fastest growing areas of Greater Cincinnati.

Right, Mainstrasse Village in historic Covington, Kentucky.

Cincinnati's skyline forms a backdrop for the Lovell-Graziani House, Covington, 1877.

Right, St. Xavier Church, Sycamore Street, built in 1860.

Procter & Gamble World Headquarters and Gardens.

Clydesdale horses, Findlay Market opening-day parade.

Octoberfest, Cincinnati.

Following pages, six bridges span the Ohio River at Cincinnati.

Summerfair at Old Coney.

Right, Taste of Cincinnati, an event to sample the food of local restaurants.
Cincinnatus mural in the background.

Following pages, Light-Up Cincinnati taken from high atop Mt. Adams.

James A. Garfield, Piatt Park.

Fredrick H. Alms Memorial Park.

St. Peter in Chains Cathedral, built in 1845.

Convention Center entry with flowers.

Carew Tower, Omni Netherland Plaza Hotel, and the Central Trust Tower.

Right, the elegant Palm Court, Omni Netherland Plaza Hotel.

John A. Roebling Suspension Bridge, opened in 1867.

Left, Skyline at twilight.

Findlay Market, named for Gen. James Findlay.

Aerial view of downtown Cincinnati and the Ohio River.

Left, St. Francis DeSales Church, Walnut Hills.

Campbell County Court House, Newport, Kentucky.

Sycamore Street in Over-the-Rhine.

Main Street in historic Over-the-Rhine is home to a popular entertainment district.

The Diner.

Right, Maisonette.

The Waterfront Restaurant.

Ohio River fog.

Right, coal barge on the Ohio River.

The Nienaber House, Covington, Kentucky. This Italianate town house was built before the Civil War.

Historic Riverside Drive, Covington, Kentucky.

James Bradley.

Right, International Street, Kings Island.

The Bicentennial Parade, Fifth Street, celebrating the city's 200th birthday.

Left, Christmas in Fountain Square.

Following page, Flying Pigs, model of Ohio River with dams, Sawyer Point Park.